Something Stirred

In search of greenness

Bob Woodroofe

Greenwood Press

First published in 2007

This impression published 2019

Greenwood Press
38 Birch Avenue
Evesham
Worcs. WR11 1YJ
Tel 01386 446477
http://greenwoodpress.co.uk

ISBN 978-0-9521165-7-8

Introduction

*this collection is to celebrate nature and the spirit of
the greenman who is still out there somewhere.*

Dedication

to Susie for her love & constant Inspiration.

It has to be

of blade of leaf of field of tree

*I am shown amazon everglade pistachio sushi lime
but do not envy these*

*long may I be swathed in endless shades
of moss apple holly sage and forest*

for these are truly green

Contents

Alien

I gaze down
below has been christianised for centuries
but forever different underneath
where the energy courses

they are foreign to her nature
she speaks the words of wisdom
opens the door to the out of doors
claws back unto her own

my branch and leaf reach
to turn us back to wildness
I will not be swayed
by the incessant talk of missionaries

that roam abroad their accusations
recriminations be stilled I stand
as I have always stood straight and true
unbowed upholding the true truth

if only they would listen
if only they had the vision to see
that it is other than their own
that they are the foreigners

Verge

caught in the corners of eyes
that flash past the endless stream
quests for speed that leads to the brink of rage
no paths in this in-between no care in this no-mans land
carnage bordered in green red mince bodies spread on
unyielding rubbered black picked at by magpie and crow

scurvy grass swarms at the edges in search of salt
coiled black vipers writhe in undergrowth
over discarded road signs men at work laid to rest
home to the black rubbish bag CBL can McD plastic tray
decapitated street tree yet beyond the barrier
under lamp post 1679's yellow glow

the squat bletted buddhas of fat frost burned hips
meditate those passing rabbit fox and badger run
dandelion and daisy flower squirrels busy themselves
on a contorted hazel amongst budding purple catkins
coppice stools shoot and chestnut buds
already sticky wait their turn

Chettewynde *

stumbling in the dark before vision I first found it
many times it lost direction petered out or was barred
then widened to a faint track that showed ahead
opening at last onto a winding path

I reached a stile slid between flat stones the way led on
through field and wood to another where I stood
and stared climbed over down into a lane
hollowed by the feet of time

not having any directions I asked people passing
'Is this the way' they said 'Yes straight on'
so I followed with heavy tread against my will
over the many bridges still to cross

came to a gate invitingly open on which I leant
rested awhile unsure then stepped through
onto a road that stretched on and promised much
its metalled glint like gold but it was fools

unhappy here I could not stay did not need to ask
knew the way leaving my possessions strewn behind
I turned aside shut the gate for ever
returned to nature's ways

** Chettywynde - Anglo-Saxon for winding path*

Fougou

comb the ground north of the Lizard
search for a souterrain
search until found

step down the worn stone slabs
the passage lit by shafts of sunlight
drop into the deep dark and quiet
a ridge stumbles you over the threshold
returns you to the womb

earth energy focused by exclusion
this house hides well its secrets
storage or refuge worship even
there is no one who knows

in the hushed tomb the sound seems loud
a rustle no a rattle repeated
echoes around off the flat stone walls
makes it hard to track down

home in get closer
then in a chink of light
a peacock butterfly vibrates its wings
warms its body before flight
up from the dark
out into the light

A drab grey sign

stares across wasteland
proclaims 'Breathing Space'
design & build packages
mushroom industrial units
concrete over earth
cram the space
that was nothing
but it was there
the breath exhaled
squashed from body
fuels consumer greed
token green lung
a vacuum within
the enclosed space
of confined minds
a dumping ground
for the dross that
society coughs up

Mayday

holloways cut deep into the moors edge
through a churchyard alight with dandelions
the path leads off across fields yellow with
vanilla gorse and celandine stars

the tiny meadow graced by ladies smock
violets hide under the hedgebank
a bumblebee drones above the rivers rush
the robin sings a welcome

here at beltane held in a cup of blackthorn froth
water trickles into the basin
sunlit ripples strobe across the surface
meditate sky and cloud

the hand reaches to the fern clothed well
crosses the sanctity of time
holds the purity of water
the energy that meets here

links the past to now
stretches forward into the future
the lichened stones hold the presence
the spirit that pours peace into the land

First light

the snake flickers
dazzles in the dark
eyes wide open
seeing nothing
going nowhere
the endless current
follows the leader
down the wire

commuters coil
nose to tail
in futile pursuit
trying to plug into
the money circuit
connect to the grid
generate wealth

as dawn dips
into day they dim
head to side
splutter and fade
wink out as
the spark dies

Cathedral

through a window see
stained shades of green
of grass blade tree leaf
folded sheep hills hem in
ridge and furrow crease the brow

brown of track weaves
grey ditch water darns
hedges knit the fields
sewn by stream's silver thread
stitching the jigsaw pieces tight

view the quilt's patchwork scene
communion between nature
and the hand of man
the heavy weight of fabric
lies lightly on the land

In a quiet garden

deep in the apple tree a wren
picks greenfly from fresh leaves
almost hidden on the bark chip path
a baby blackbird with speckled breast
sunbathes with beak agape panting

robin dunnock and flycatcher
all live in harmony here
amongst this garden's bounty
where the water always flows
clean and pure from the well

last night we climbed the tor
sat and watched the sun drop
below purpled banks of cloud
gazed until it sank down out
of sight behind brent knoll

until spots before our eyes
and peace in our hearts
we stumbled down the hill
into the darkness
heading for home

Erme row

to the south they stand
on a moor named after a river
that lives up to its name
row upon row of reaves

follow their lichen encrusted tops
that poke above the bracken
they lead you on and on
out across the vastness

away from the sheltered valley
after whose river they are named
once there came a strange procession
to lay down their dead

into the tumulus on the tor
crowned by a rocky cairn
to look out over this ancient land
to guard it for the new

Regeneration

they have prettied the river
piled the banks tarmaced the paths
contained it all by regimented iron railings
the old ponds that once rang to the thrash of
mini paddles and children's cries now dormant
one a flower garden the other
blanketed in weed full of debris
token sculptures rise from groundcover
eof's bronze creation still to come

the wildflower meadow blooms
arches filled with cold metal versions
still the waterfowl come for their daily bread
still the boats the trippers
another piece of urbanised countryside
easily accessible to all
with full facilities to hand
spoiled

Joseph

under the canopy of mist a barge
slices the duckweed coated channel
slides silently along the rhyne
only the rustle of reeds
edging the cut
marks its passage
push and lift push and lift
even the drip of water from the pole
sounds out across the levels

there is no course to steer
through these liquid wastes
without land to be seen
appease the gods offer a sword
to slice through these dark waters
cut away the mist find and follow
the track that leads to land
know it is here this is the way
be still and wait - wait

the veil lifts a terrace appears
rises slowly another looms
still another emerges from the gloom
feet on solid earth
grounded now
plant my staff that it may grow

Cathedral

aisle leads to sheltering dome
risen from buttress rooted rock
smooth boles strain upward
branch tracery touches sky
pointed buds finger light

queued from the far horizon
an endless pilgrim procession
passes the ancient tomb
bedded in leaves of gold

black grey white all mourn
pay homage pass on along
the path of heavens avenue
across timeless roll of down
open distance into space

air and light is in me now
freedom reaches in
stretches to eternity

Over the weekend

in the space of sunshine after rain
dark weals scar the sward
livid tracks carve the ground
stark white vans in green oasis
whine of generators cutting quiet
violation of this place of peace
miss-spelt signs proclaim innocence
but the broken laws remain
the long wait for the powers to serve
the inevitable media circus
till they limp away in the rain
convoy down the glistening road
let the light flow in once more

Solstice – Ring of Brodgar

the clamour of black-headed gulls
and calling curlews
the sun drops below the bank of cloud
that hangs to the north west
illuminates that side of the stones
the reverse in black shadow
earlier a rainbow had spanned
the space between two stones
linked with light for a moment
ten thirty pm and the sun
sinks below the horizon
the ring is alive with people
hushed in quiet contemplation
come to celebrate the season
as the earth journeys on
the oyster catchers
pipe in the heart of summer

Summer Solstice

rain in the wind we climb the tor
rocks in the rain pocketed hollows
dished water for the traveller
lichen and rocks inching over
skies cloud over lichen sweep across
mist under sky lingers
young stream heard but not seen
stone slabs stacked waiting

yesterday sparkling blue white foam
gulls adrift on thermals
green flash of hairstreak
steps steep down the cliff
jumble of rocks crumpled slate
black white and between
tumbled by the tide
every conceivable shade

Seekers

they sought to plant in the green of fields
under the paleness of an English sun
to grow alongside the famous plum
next to the mountain of waste
where the gulls clamour and wheel
and the diggers turn the steaming
rows that stretch for miles
the ribbons of colour rainbow
dance along the perimeter wire
next to the hooves that no longer run
where the bleating mouths are stilled
sealed with the heaviness of lias clay
capped with the good English earth
seeping seeping down and away

Further north

It's already light
the sky lit by pink cloud
and plane trails

shoes dampen with dew
as we push through grass
larks soar over green ears of wheat

we expect you to rise over the abbey
but you surprise us
when you appear over the hill

we are humbled
by our lack of knowledge
as we hurtle round you

yet you still reward us
with your presence
to grace our day once more

Screw

each day turn a little further away
from standard towards that indefinite space
somewhere between man and nature
some would say the spiral of mid-life crisis
brought on by divorce redundancy but no
it's always been there under the surface
smouldering like a deep peatland burn
trapped in life's helix it erupts now and then
has to worm a way out have its head
can you tap it put it into words
what creates it drives it along
controls it as the thread tightens
who turns the screwdriver
just know that you must you will
as you drive towards your goal

Dancing at Lughnasa

follow the dusty footsteps
along the old old road
flanked with flowers and butterflies
to the grove where the smithy lingers

huge stones frame the entrance
the long slope of the barrow
tapers away to the north
to where a woman dances

in flowing white gown
barefoot on the grass
to the black clad pipers air
that flutes over beech cool whisper

notes fade into the hum of summer
the lone voice tells of the endless journey
the blade is drawn and raised
to mark this time - here - now
celebrate the gift of plenty

Viriditas *

all around he coils and twines
in stone and wood creeps and climbs
on church and tower watching over
father son lover of earth mother
he rises on the eve of may
celebrates new life
by halloween work done
he rests thus balancing the year

reborn from the wood
green spirits speak to man
of natures common sense
rooted deep in earth
the words are leaves
they rise with the sap
carved from his heart the
message spreads on the wind

leaf and head must be close
sleep and wake
work together
learn together
once he was alone
then we were his
then we took over
now we must be one

**Viriditas, a word meaning Greenness, created by
Hildegard of Bingen, a12th Century German Nun.*

Glendalough*

ageless antiquity
layer upon layer
stone upon stone
builds this place of worship

air is heavy with quiet day
moisture hangs still
damp drips through peat and stone
steeps green blade and frond

clouded mountains humble
rock ridges edged by pine
reflect immense mouths
teeth sunk in mirrored lake

midges smoke water
rings of feeding fish spread
die in the vastness of calm
a crow caws the silence

** Monastic settlement in the Wicklow mountains of
Ireland founded by St. Kevin in the 11th Century.*

Watchers

24 hour feeding stations
constantly consuming
the daily drudge of life
perched on high
they crane forward
stilt legged snapping
at the passing hordes
of multi coloured ants
that crawl along
the ribbon of life
a ceaseless stream
of lights throb
one way white
the other red
nose to tail at speed
the looped neck of cable
always full of sky
you never see the bulge
of the constantly taken
meal slipping down

Search

you and I
searched
we found

brown velvet in short turf in cool spring wind
shared midsummer cushions with Clare
saw curled tails on tall stems race across the heath
walked in Jefferies footsteps under azure skies
tiny spirals white in grassy rings under sun's autumn glare
touched engraved chalk wall coldness under busy street
felt earth energy flow through body hand and rod
dined on the sweet food of love on rolling down
heard calmness descend from the tor bubble from spring

we searched
we nearly found
you and I

Something stirred

through the dust of cars
chaos of crowds
the grub of money
he re-appears

spans the world
measures with sticks
like the dodman
and the ley

antlers adorn his head
beneath a mask
leaves of green
benign or cruel

tell me
is it now

Walkabout

down the dreaming tracks
spirit children linger
in the footprints of ancestors
poets of your own creation
you sang the world into existence

sacred to the wandering tribe
the tune remains the same
words haze and mingle
cross boundaries and borders
map the contours of your land

earth gives forth life eternal
wound the earth wound yourself
that is the way of the land
It takes you back when you die
go back in dream time

follow your own song line
search for pasture
where you do not have to ask
to be at home and yet
are free to leave

Knowlton

sun beats on the chase the henge is small
holds something intangible saxons tried to sanctify it
their church lies in ruins

bank and ditch hem in the feeling you can't define
brown of parasitic broomrape drains flower filled banks
adds an alien feel to the scene

'look for artefacts in molehills' the archaeologist said
I delve deep into warm earth and unearth a tooth
human but whose and how old

we have come here to test the rods
cool metal lies in palms sticky with sweat
can we discern whatever it is that lies here

respond to the energy the force transmit it
through fingers slippery on the elemental copper
held in front balanced and still

cross the circle concentrate - feel for it
whatever it is this unknown entity
at the junction of bank and ditch they

tremble slowly turn inward and cross
my fingers tingle I know it is not my doing
the hairs on the back of my neck stand

Long Man

we came to see you when combines roamed
the fields sucking in the glowing corn
spouting plumes of chaff that fell
from molten sky to drape the hedges

what you stood for then remains
under your gaze still being gathered in
blazed white into green you lie longer than
you look taller than the eye perceives

the long steady trudge uphill to
your feet the outline fainter here
where other feet have eroded
but we will not set foot on you

we will skirt up the rising down
to reach and drink your daily view
and there as we climb the stile
autumn tresses in your hair

Pity the heart

uprooted carried piece by piece
you rest here brown and worn
cloistered north and south of aisle
in this house of prayer
coloured by winter light
filtered through stained glass
your earthy hues glow warm
polished by time and habit
touch smooth and rounded grain
feel centuries awaken ghosts
of monk and caroller who
grateful stood and leant
slowly smoothed you down
flowers beasts George and dragon
noble heads wreaths of laurel
green men speaking leaves
shiel-na-gigs ward of the devil
heads dreamt these designs
hands shaped them
fingered tools that cut them in
only mind maps
carved in wood remain

RIP

deep inside nature's gutter
gutted by tooth and talon
a blizzard of foul words barked
visceral language the gore of life
splattered over pure pages

drawn by a howling moon
from black suck of bog
the oily swirl of fast water
through lank matted grass
the slink of wood shadow

in the wan light of eclipsed sun
mind driven by bestial urge
inherited down a blood line
stands man the animal
fouling his own nest

you plunged over the edge
through all this mayhem
bloodshot into the void
into the beauty and peace
that will always be there

Wodewove*

quiet across the woodland glade
comes the woodman with his blade
soon to ring through tree and wood
bleed away the sap like blood
like my crop I grow straight and true
my strength of character runs right through
I too am just as green as they
with leaves about my faces
I love to work and lie and dream
in amongst their shady places
there I sing my own sweet song
and whistle tunes upon the air
they hear me safe within their homes
and from deep inside their lair
they never see me yet they know
who I am and what I stand for
I come from the deepest wildwood
still uphold its ancient law
my mother wouldn't know me
because I am not of her alone
I belong in hedge and wood
rise through earth and stone
shrouded in green monk's habit
guardian spirits hasten to the task
shadows behind the trunk
hidden by the mask
forever upon the woodland scene
my name is Mr. Green

** Wodewove - dark man of the woods*

Winter Solstice

the rose glow of warning pinks a cold sky
a reluctant sun sulks behind the hills
creamed clouds float westward over the stillness
broken by the mistle searching the yew
every pluck showers rime into the air
onto grass crisp under white grasp of frost
the resident blackbirds spar amongst a
mess of leaves that adhere to silvered lawn
starling squadrons swoop for their daily feast
of glutinous cones red as winter sun
chuck of grey backed fieldfare echoes in quiet
a flash of redwing matches the berries
in the dawn light the huddled figures wait
to see the sun bloody the stone once more

Time

*the roundabout turns
wherever you get on or off
it is never the same
you cannot stop
there are no sides
no safety rail
only you and the world
enjoy your ride*

About the Author

Born & bred & still living in the Vale of Evesham Bob Woodroofe's poems appear in many poetry magazines & are performed locally. Inspired by the natural world, the landscape & local tradition he attempts to bring the magic of nature & its restorative & healing qualities to a wider audience.

Also available from the

Greenwood Press
38 Birch Avenue
Evesham
Worcs. WR11 1YJ

website http://greenwoodpress.co.uk

e-mail info@greenwoodpress.co.uk

by Bob Woodroofe

A trilogy of poetry collections from
life & nature in the Vale of Evesham

Nature, Reflections & Spirit of the Vale

In search of greenness

Something Stirred

the Poetry Collection

Pick of the crop

Joint poetry collections by
Sue Johnson & Bob Woodroofe

Tales of Trees *&* **Journey**

Creative Writing books
by Sue Johnson

Writer's Toolkit & Writer's Toolkit 2, 3 & 4